Learn to Read and Write
SECRET MESSAGES in

Ancient Egyptian Hieroglyphs

This book belongs to:

_____

Thank you for your purchase!
We'd love to hear how you
enjoyed this product. Please
take a moment to leave us your
feedback in the review section
of Amazon.

Special thanks to our friends at Dreamstime.com

What are hieroglyphs?

Hieroglyphs are an ancient Egyptian form of writing that were developed more than 5000 years ago. These included over 6000 different pictures or symbols used to represent ideas and sounds. In this book, however, we will simply use symbols that represent our own alphabet.

Hieroglyphics were considered sacred. Only about 3% of the population knew how to read and write them - mainly scribes, priests, royalty, and the stone carvers who actually cut the symbols into the temple and tomb walls. Everyone else had a different form of writing that they used.

Unlike our own modern languages, the ancient Egyptians did not put spaces between words, sentences or paragraphs. Nor did they use punctuation at the end of sentences. They rarely used vowels. This made reading hieroglyphics very difficult.

They would also write them vertically and horizontally, and from both left-to-right and right-to-left. You could tell which way to read based on what direction the symbol was facing. For example - if the nose of the lion is pointed left, it should be read from left-to-right. If the nose is pointing right, then you read from right-to-left.

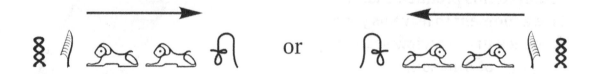

Now that you have a basic understanding of what they are, let's get started so you can write your own messages in ancient Egyptian hieroglyphs!

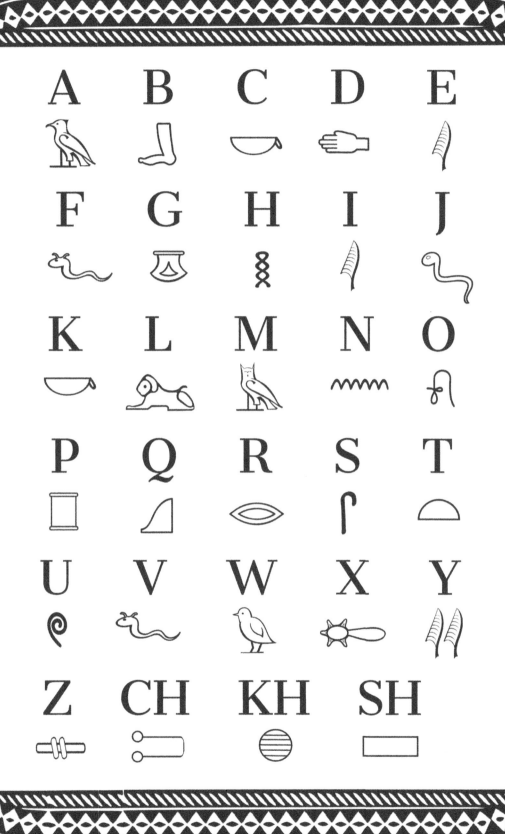

The Vulture

Color each of the hieroglyphs as you go along!

Now you try!

Trace the images and then draw your own.

A

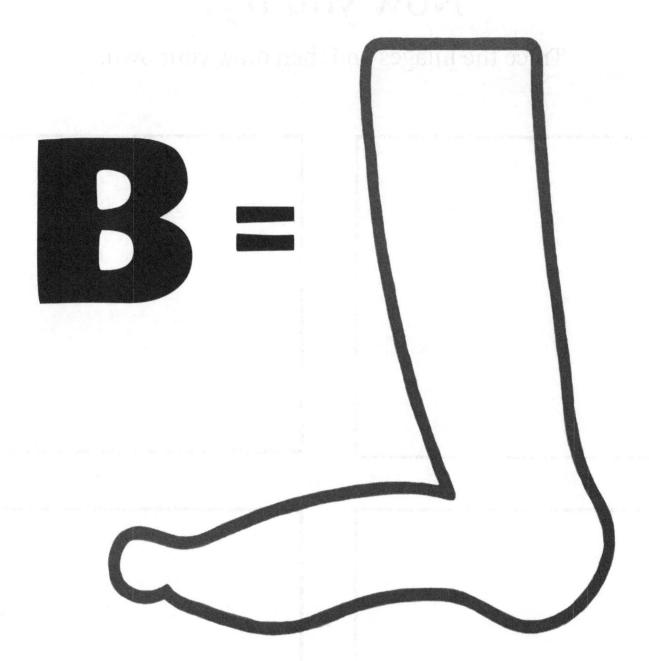

The Lower Leg

Fun Fact: Men, women and children all shaved their heads bald in ancient Egypt. It is thought that because of lice, they preferred to go bald or wear wigs.

Now you try!

Trace the images and then draw your own.

B

Now you try!

Trace the images and then draw your own

= C or K

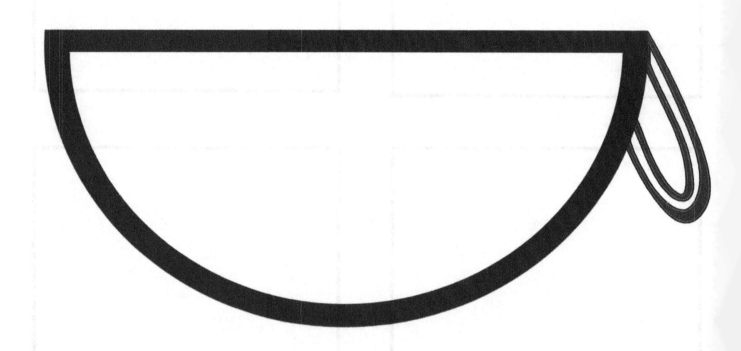

The Basket

Now you try!

Trace the images and then draw your own.

c

D =

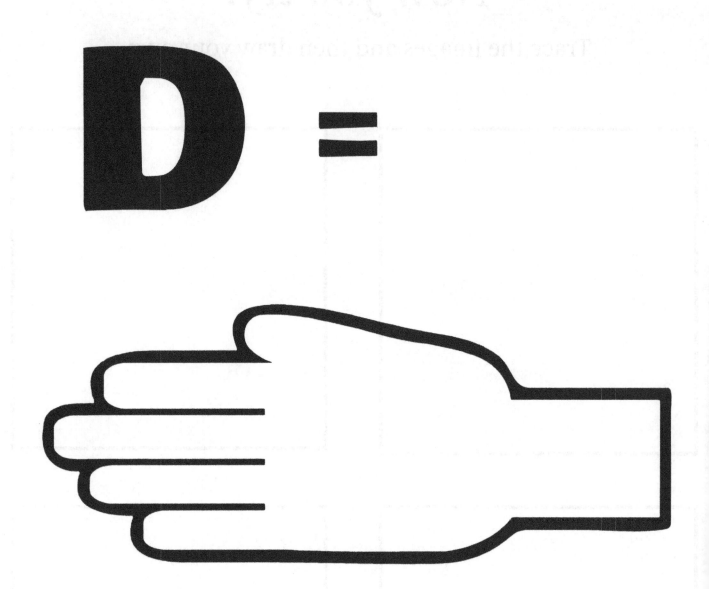

The Hand

Fun fact: Both men and women also wore make-up.

Now you try!

Trace the images and then draw your own.

D

E or I =

The Feather

Now you try!

Trace the images and then draw your own.

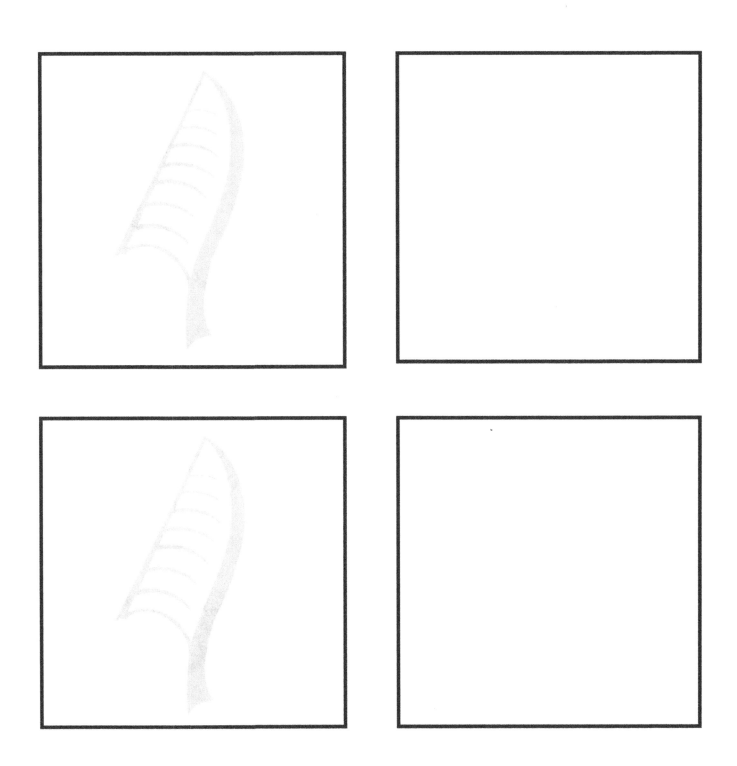

E

Alphabet Match

Write the letter (A,B,C,D,E) next to its correct symbol. Then draw a line from the hieroglyph on the left to the picture on the right that starts with that letter.

Using the symbols you have learned, what word does this spell?

 _____

Connect the Dots and Color!

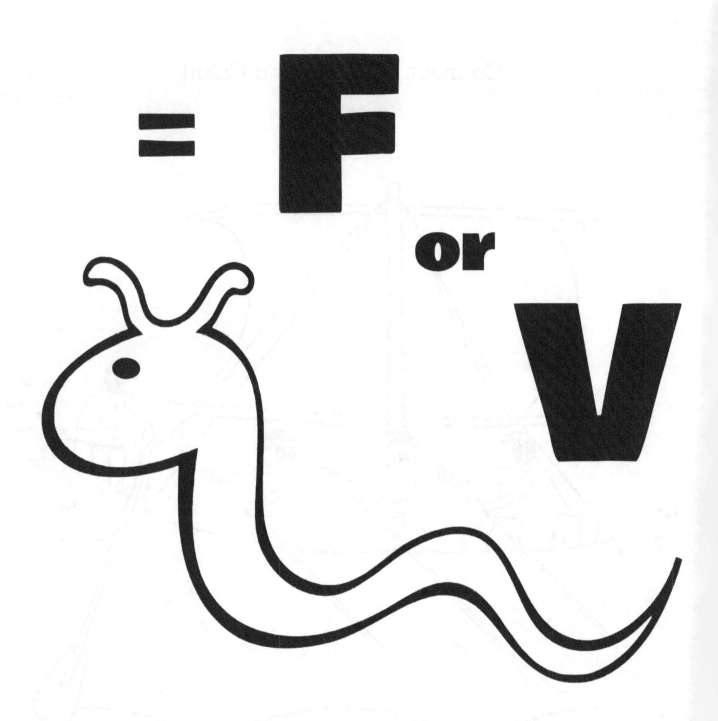

The Viper

Fun fact: Tutankhamun (King Tut) became pharaoh at just 9 years old.

Now you try!

Trace the images and then draw your own.

F

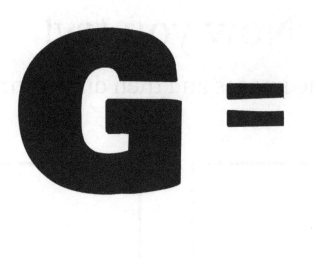

The Pot

Now you try!

Trace the images and then draw your own.

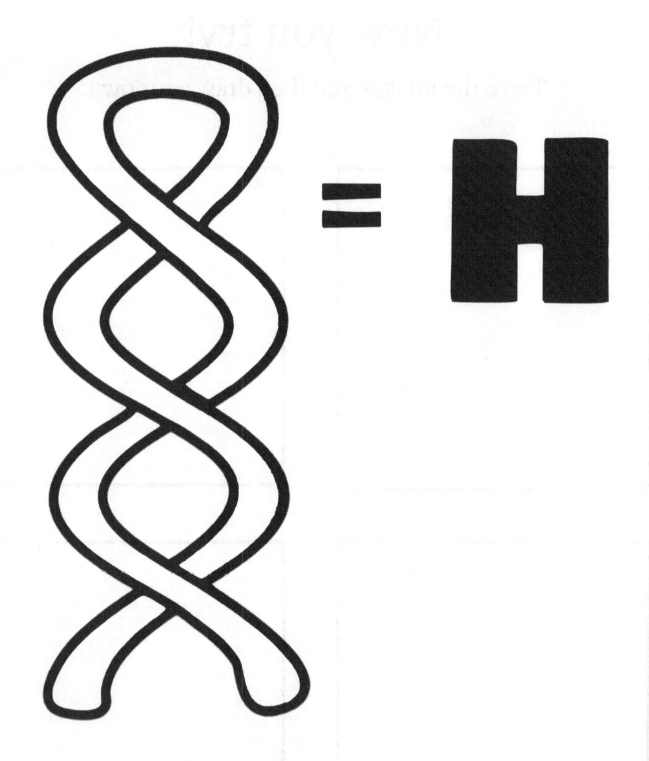

The Wick

Fun fact: Bathrooms were built in some of the temples for the pharaoh to use in the afterlife.

Now you try!

Trace the images and then draw your own.

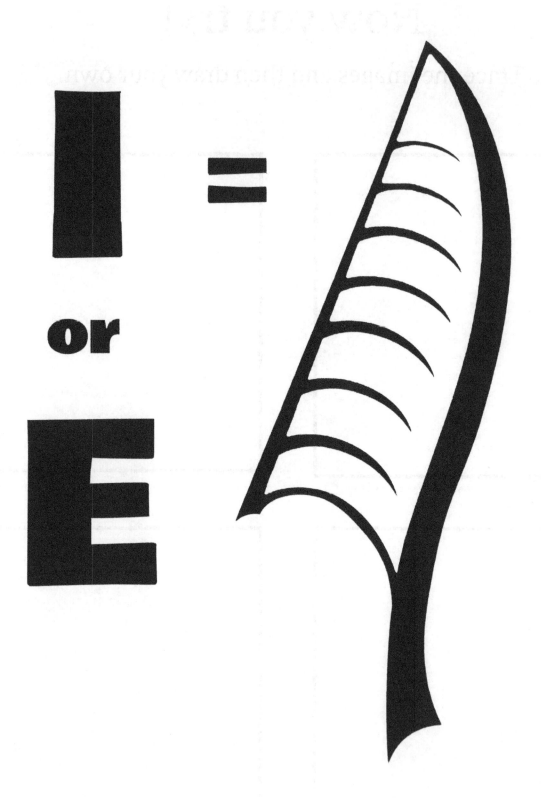

The Feather

Now you try!

Trace the images and then draw your own.

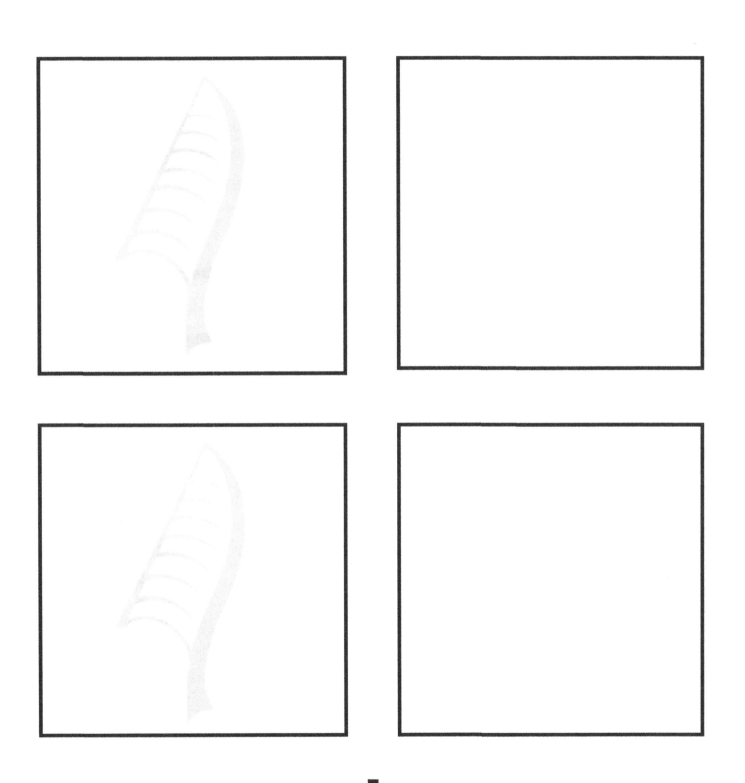

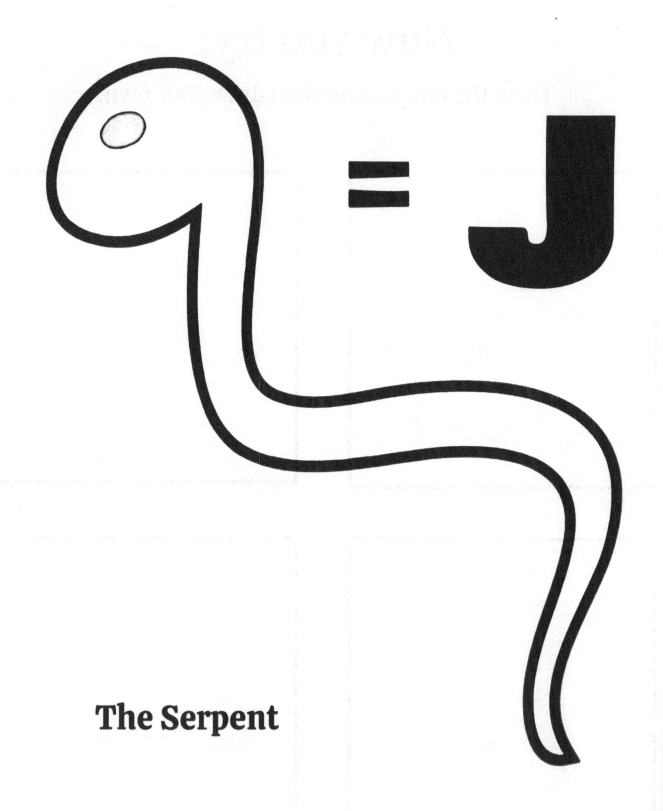

The Serpent

Fun Fact: The Great Pyramid of Giza is the only one remaining of the 7 Wonders of the Ancient World.

Now you try!

Trace the images and then draw your own.

J

Alphabet Match

Write the letter (F,G,H,I,J) on the dash next to its correct symbol. Then draw a line from the hieroglyph to the picture that starts with that letter.

Using the symbols you have learned, what word does this spell?

Find the Difference

Look at the images below and circle the one that is different from the others.

= **K** or **C**

The Basket

Now you try!

Trace the images and then draw your own.

The Lion

Fun fact: Cleopatra, Queen of Egypt, spoke 12 different languages.

Now you try!

Trace the images and then draw your own.

L

The Owl

Now you try!

Trace the images and then draw your own.

The Water

Fun fact: It is thought that the Egyptians invented toothpaste, but not in the flavors we know today. They used ashes, burnt egg shells and crushed ox hooves to brush their teeth.

Now you try!

Trace the images and then draw your own.

N

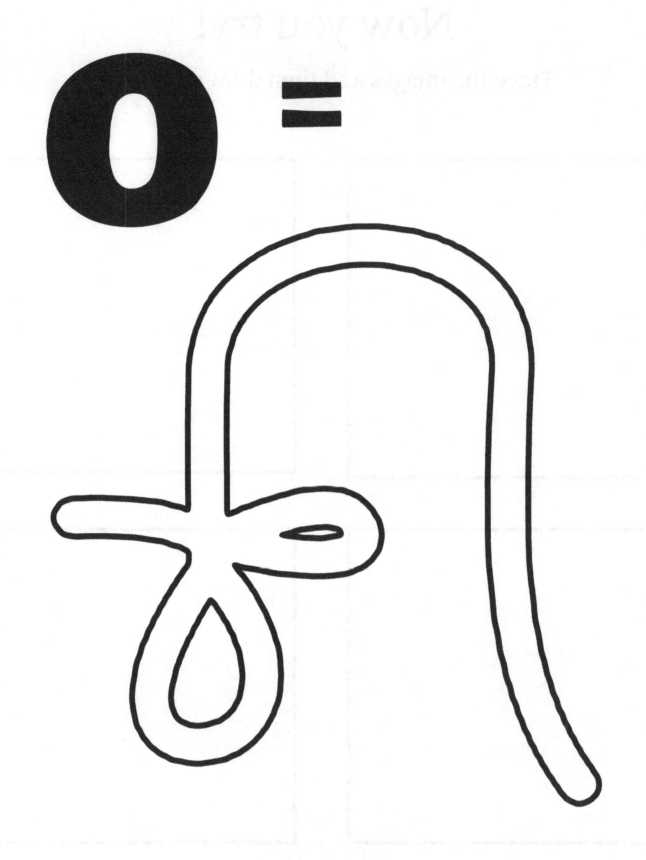

The Lasso

Now you try!

Trace the images and then draw your own.

0

Alphabet Match

Write the letter (K,L,M,N,O) next to its correct symbol. Then draw a line from the hieroglyph to the picture that starts with that letter.

Using the symbols you have learned, what word does this spell?

_____

Find the words on the list in the word search area and circle them.
Words can be forward, backward, vertical or diagonal.

```
A B Z R E D H G O A
H D I S C O V E R F
W I V L A R I V E R
P M A E A N W A E I
A A E A N A D A G C
P R M Y S T E R Y A
Y Y R E E D U A P X
R P G Y A X S R T J
U C H A R I O T E K
S P H I N X L Q A U
```

Africa
discover
sand
adventure

mystery
Egypt
river
pyramid

chariot
reed
sphinx
papyrus

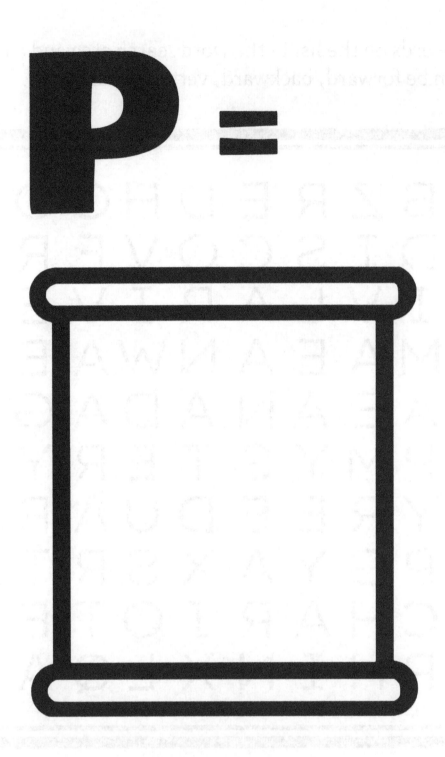

The Stool

Fun fact: Ancient Egyptians loved playing board games, so much so that games were often buried with them.

Now you try!

Trace the images and then draw your own.

P

Q =

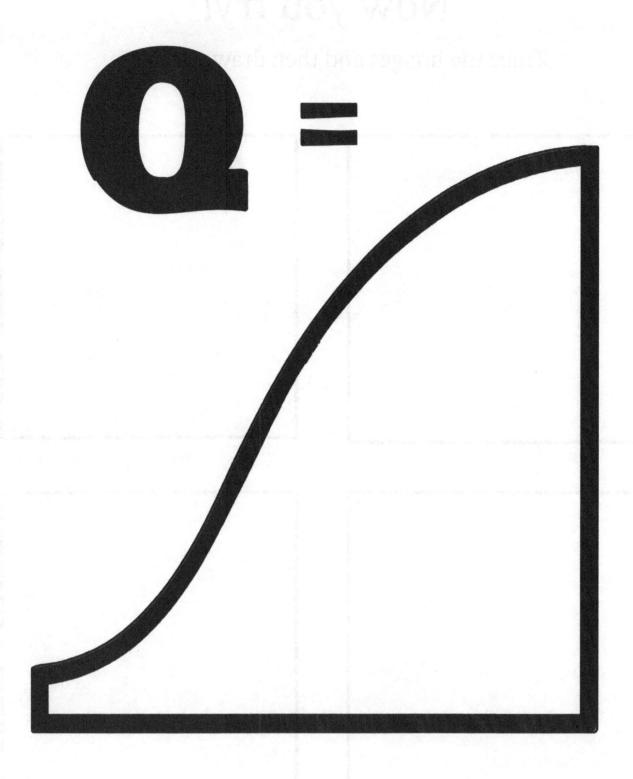

The Hill

Now you try!

Trace the images and then draw your own.

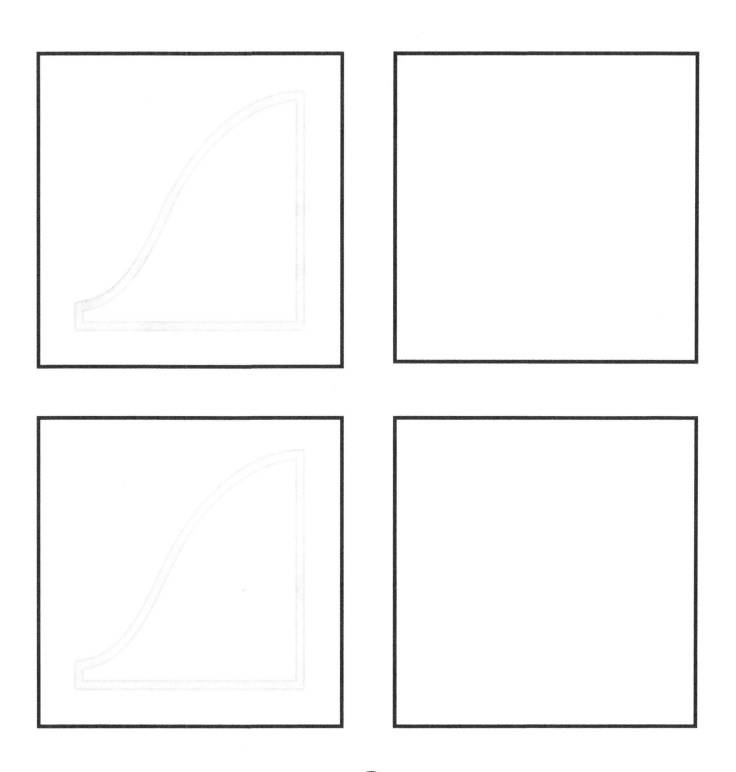

Q

R =

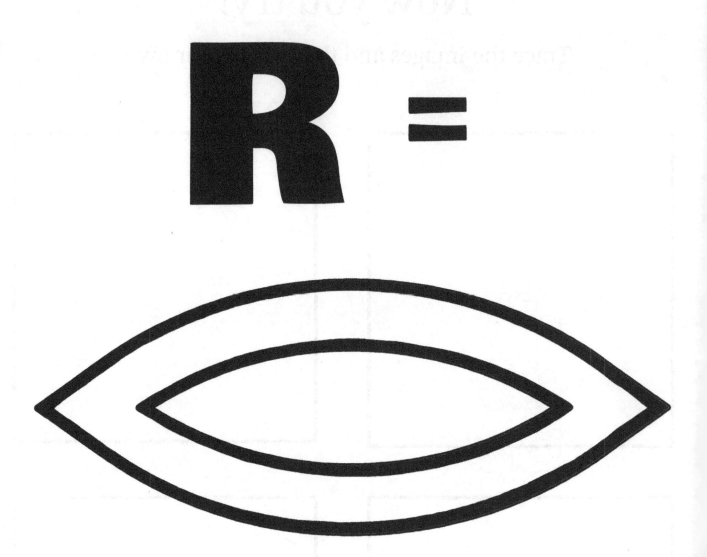

The Mouth

Fun fact: The dagger found wrapped in the linens of King Tut's mummy was made out of a meteorite that fell from the sky. The iron of this blade was considered to be more valuable than gold.

Now you try!

Trace the images and then draw your own.

R

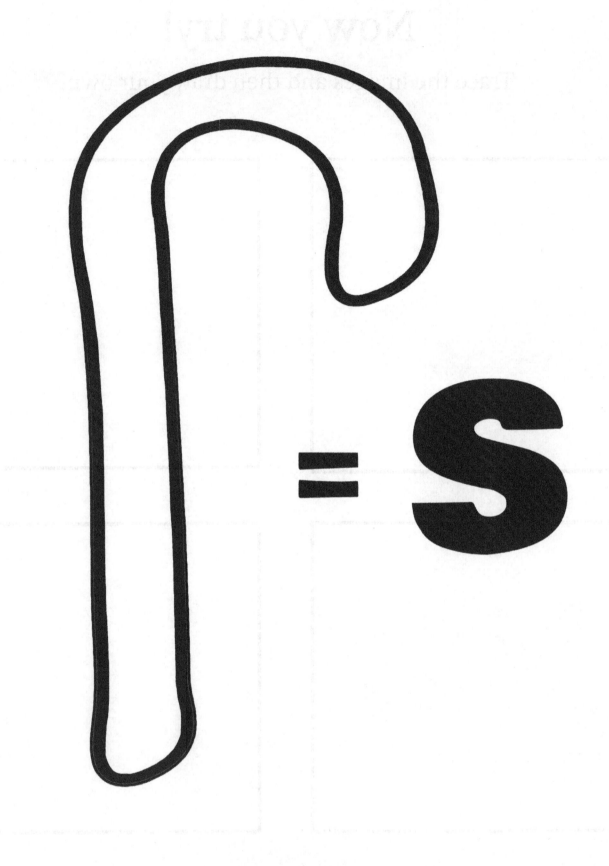

The Cloth

Now you try!

Trace the images and then draw your own.

s

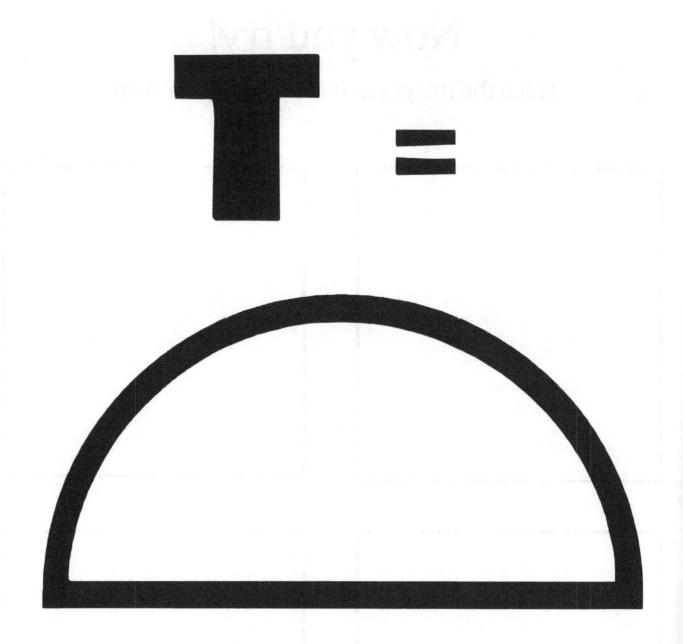

The Loaf of Bread

Fun fact: The pyramids of Giza were originally covered in polished white limestone so that they gleamed in the sunlight. The limestone fell off during an earthquake and the stones were later taken away to be used for other buildings.

Now you try!

Trace the images and then draw your own.

T

Alphabet Match

Write the letter (P,Q,R,S,T) on the dash next to its correct symbol. Then draw a line from the hieroglyph to the picture that starts with that letter.

Using the symbols you have learned, what word does this spell?

Help these 2 friends find each other!

Lotus Flower

The Rope

Now you try!

Trace the images and then draw your own.

U

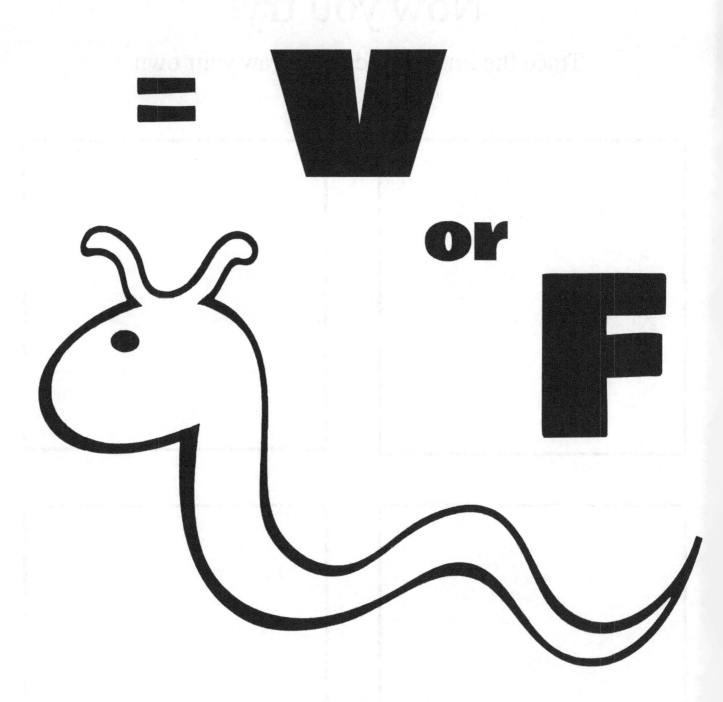

The Viper

Fun fact: Eygpt is home to over 130 pyramids.

Now you try!

Trace the images and then draw your own.

v

The Chick

Now you try!

Trace the images and then draw your own.

X =

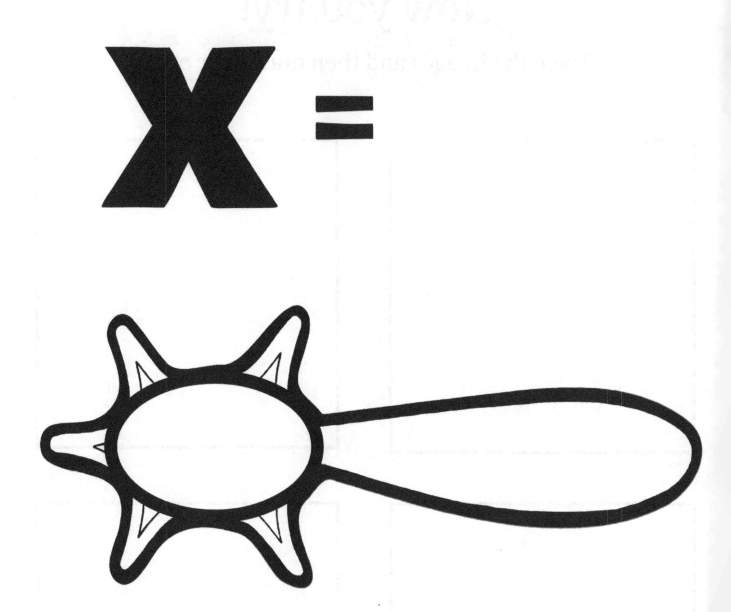

The Animal Tail

Fun fact: Ancient Egyptians loved having pets. Cats and monkeys were among their favorites.

Now you try!

Trace the images and then draw your own.

X

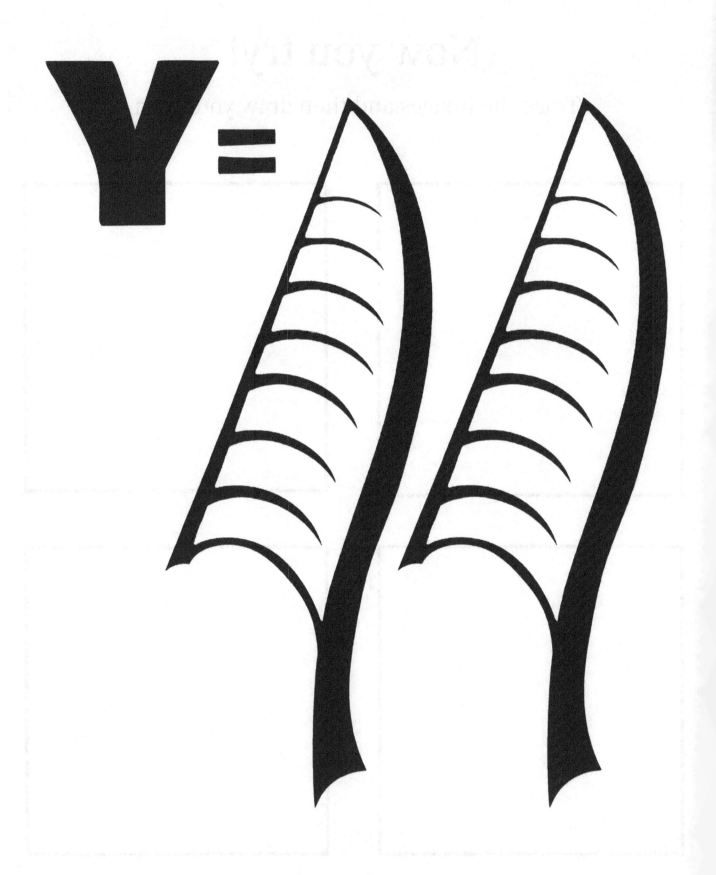

Two Feathers

Now you try!

Trace the images and then draw your own.

Y

Alphabet Match

Write the letter (U,V,W,X,Y) on the dash next to its correct symbol. Then draw a line from the hieroglyph to the picture that starts with that letter.

Using the symbols you have learned, what word does this spell?

Use the gird to help you draw the other half of King Tut.

Pharaoh Tutankhanum

Z =

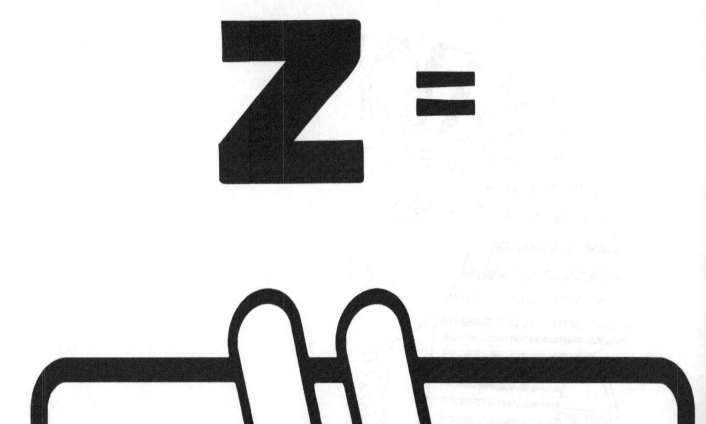

The Bolt

Fun fact: The Egyptians would use moldy bread to help heal their cuts. It wasn't until 2000 years later that Alexander Fleming discovered penicillin, the medicine we use today, on moldy bread.

Now you try!

Trace the images and then draw your own.

z

CH =

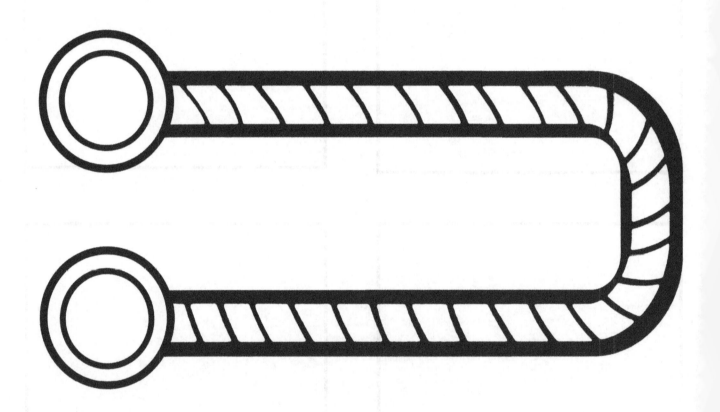

The Tether Cord

Now you try!

Trace the images and then draw your own.

CH

KH =

The Sieve

Fun fact: The woolly mammoth, cousin to the modern elephant, was still alive when the pyramids at Giza were being built. They went extinct about 4000 years ago.

Now you try!

Trace the images and then draw your own.

SH =

The Pool

Fun fact: Egyptians aligned the pyramids of Giza exactly to the stars that make up the belt in the constellation Orion.

Now you try!

Trace the images and then draw your own.

Alphabet Match

Write the letters (Z, CH, KH, SH) on the dash next to its correct symbol. Then draw a line from the hieroglyph to the picture that starts with that letter.

Using the symbols you have learned, what word does this spell?

_____

Cartouche

A cartouche, or "shenu" is an oval symbol the pharaoh and members of the royal family placed around their names to show their importance. It was also believed to help protect them and bring them good luck.

Congratulations! You can now write in hieroglyphs! YOU are important too! So draw your name in hieroglyphs in this cartouche. Start at the top and go down.

Help this little girl find her papyrus.

Reminder!

The letters C and K use the same symbol - ⌣
As do E and I - ∥   and F and V - 𓆓

Keep this in mind whenever you are translating from hieroglyphics to English. When you see one of these symbols, remember it could be one letter or the other. It might make it easier to decipher the word if you sometimes translate the other letters around it first. Then try both letters to see which one makes the most sense.

Example - look at this sentence in hieroglyphs:

could mean "quiin, quien, quein or queen.
Which word makes the most sense? Circle it.

could mean "quete, quiti, quite, or queti.
Circle the word which makes the most sense.

could mean "queet, quiet, queit, or quiit.
Circle the word which makes the most sense.

When you choose the words that make the most sense, then so does the sentence they form. Did you figure this one out?

It reads: "The queen got quite quiet."

Now you try! What does this word mean?

Answer:

Translate

the words that are in English into hieroglyphs.

1. shy   _____ _____

2. dog   ____ ____ ____

3. bike   ____ ____ ____ ____

4. jump   ____ ____ ____ ____

5. ocean   ____ ____ ____ ____ ____

6. paint   ____ ____ ____ ____ ____

7. horse   ____ ____ ____ ____ ____

8. glove   ____ ____ ____ ____ ____

9. porch   ____ ____ ____ ____ ____

10. waffle   ____ ____ ____ ____ ____

Translate
the words that are in hieroglyphs into English.

1.  _____

2. _____

3. _____

4. _____

5. _____

6. _____

7. _____

8. _____

9. _____

10. _____

Translate the words in hieroglyphics. Then find the English meaning in the word search area and circle it. Words can be forward, backward, vertical or diagonal.

```
T G Z B E L P W O J
Q H I S C A M E L S
V M R L H R U V I F
N A A O O N W G E B
I T B F N S D A G S
L I E Y E E E R C A
E J R M Y B U R P X
O Z A U P T O M B S
H G H R Q L V T E D
M W J C L X E G I Y
```

_____   _____

_____   _____

_____   _____

_____   _____

Find the Difference

Look at the images below and circle the one that is different from the others.

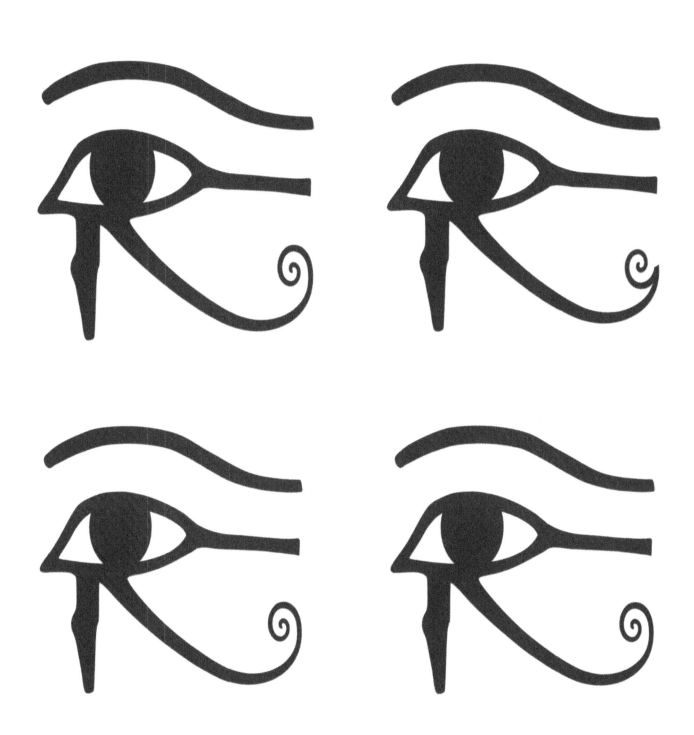

Eye of Horus

Use the gird to help you draw the other half of the beetle.

The Sacred Scarab

Find the Sphinx

Who will get there - the cat, the rat or the dog? Translate the hieroglyphs below for a clue.

‒ ‒ ‒ ‒ ‒ ‒ ‒ ‒ ‒ ‒ ‒ ‒

Translate the words from English into hieroglyphics. Then find the symbols in the word search area and circle them. Words can be forward, backward, vertical or diagonal.

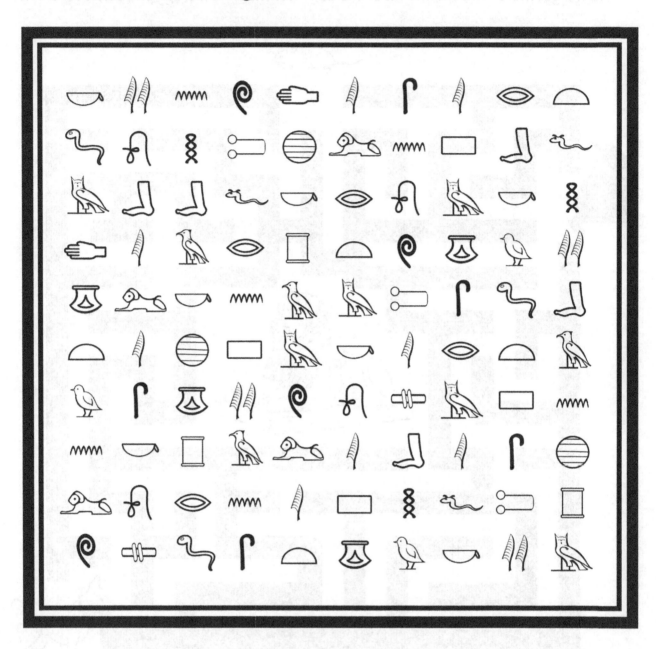

gold _____   ibis _____

mummy _____   ankh _____

obelisk _____   cobra _____

amulet _____   desert _____

Translate the words in hieroglyphics. Then find the English meaning in the word search area and circle it. Words can be forward, backward, vertical or diagonal.

```
H J S G A P T A G Z
R I I D I L Z F O M
K Z E A Z S I V D O
A H S R U L K N D N
C A R T O U C H E F
S E O I I G P G S N
I L L F P Z L L S Y
R B Z A B L O Y O M
Y I E C A L A P P K
O I A T X D E W I H
```

_____   _____

_____   _____

_____   _____

_____   _____

The Sacred Scarab has been lost! It is up to you to go into the maze, find it and return it the Pharoah who waits on the other side.

Translate the words from English into hieroglyphics. Then find the symbols in the word search area and circle them. Words can be forward, backward, vertical or diagonal.

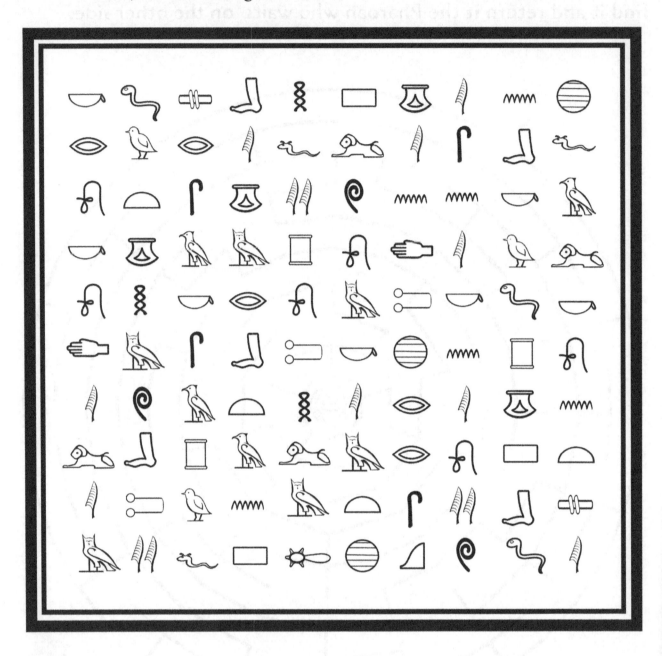

palm _____   robe _____

falcon _____   baboon _____

incense _____   silver _____

crocodile _____   archery _____

Maat - goddess of harmony and truth

My dear friend –

I have learned something exciting about the Great pyramid of Giza; something that very few people know.

Solve the following clues to see if you can discover it too.

Good luck!

HELP SOLVE THE MYSTERY OF THE GREAT PYRAMID OF GIZA

1. If the sun is in front of you, what is behind you?

2. How many arms does an octopus have?

3. If a hedgehog looks up to see the pyramid, then what does a bird flying overhead do to see it?

Answers:
1. Your shadow.
2. 8.
3. Looks down.
So what does this all add up to?

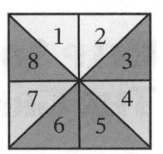

The Great Pyramid of Giza has 8 sides!

That's right! Although it appears to have a square base with just 4 sides, the Great Pyramid of Giza has 8 sides!

In 1940, a British Air Force pilot by the name of P. Groves was flying over the pyramids when he noticed something unusual about its shadows. It was very subtle, but the shadows highlighted 8 sides, not 4. You can tell by this photo he took. Do you see the line down the center of the side? You can only see this from the air, and only at certain times of the year.

Decode this message from the author!

Answer Key

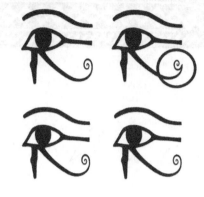

Word Search 1

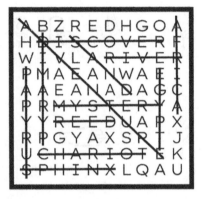

Word Search 2

Word Search 3

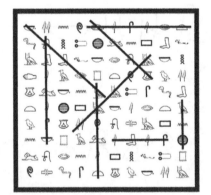

1. What does this word mean?   Fever

Translate from English to hieroglyphs...
1. shy
2. dog
3. bike
4. jump
5. ocean
6. paint
7. horse
8. glove
9. porch
10. waffle

Translate from hieroglyphs to English...
1. box 2. swim 3. joke 4. equal 5. shade
6. beach 7. funny 8. night 9. zipper 10. vanilla

Word Search 4

Word Search 5

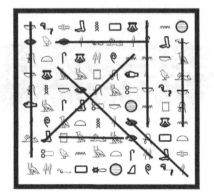

Please use these pages to write your own secret messages in ancient Egyptian hieroglyphs! Have fun!

Made in the USA
Las Vegas, NV
09 November 2024

11436626R00059